Little Bear and The Two Caves

A Children's Book About Divorce with a Parent's Guide to Help Children Understand and Talk About Divorce

Copyright 2025 LifeThreads Books Evergreen, Colorado

All rights reserved.
The material contained herein is owned by Shannon R. Rios Paulsen, MS LMFT PCC.

This book or portions thereof may not be duplicated in any form except where properly attributed under Fair Use guidelines (http://www.copyright.gov/fls/fl102.html) as permitted under United States Copyright Act of 1976.

Material may not be duplicated, distributed, or used without the expressed written permission of the author.

LifeThreads Books Evergreen, CO 80439 www.healthychildrenofdivorce.com

ISBN: 978-0-9916361-4-3

DEDICATION:

To the children of divorce:
May this be a piece of your happy and healthy childhood.

To the parents of divorce:
May this be the start of many healthy conversations
you will have with your child.

To my two magical children, Emma Emaya and Elliott:
Thank you for choosing me to be your mommy.
I am forever grateful. I love you forever.

Parent's Guide

Thank you for purchasing this book for you and your child. I have worked with thousands of children and families of divorce and separation over the last 22 years (www.healthychildrenofdivorce.com). My hope is that this book encourages open communication between you and your child, a dialogue that will continue as they grow. As a children's therapist, I have told this story to many children. I decided to write this book (during COVID-19, when I could not see children) so all parents could tell their children this story. This book is unique as it includes a parent's guide to help you be the expert as you read this story to your child. I am here with you in heart and mind as you share these important messages with your child.

This book will:
- Help you minimize the risk related to divorce/separation for your child.
- Help your children understand what divorce is and how it will impact them.
- Give you the most important questions/discussion ideas to help your child adjust.
- Provide you with insight into how your child is adjusting and what you can do to help them adjust in the best way possible.
- Begin the communication process around divorce, which is a crucial aspect of protecting your children during this time.

My passion is happy and healthy children. If you want to know more about what is best for your kids, please read one of my books on parenting and divorce. They can be found at www.healthychildrenofdivorce.com. I also coach parents (via Zoom or phone) to be the best parents possible for their children during this time of transition.

As I tell all the parents I work with, I work for your children. My only goal is healthy and happy kids. I believe this book will help ensure that your children are healthy and happy through the divorce. Thank you for putting your child first during this time. They will thank you for it. I wish your family all the love and peace in the world.

My Very Best,

Shannon Rios Paulsen MS LMFT PCC
www.healthychildrenofdivorce.com

PARENT'S GUIDE

Please go over this guide PRIOR to reading through the book with your child. It will help you add valuable information that will be helpful for them.

Your job as a parent is to be CURIOUS. If you don't know the answer to a question, let your child know that. Let them know that you will get back to them. The goal is to open up discussion between you and your child. The words in *italics* are words you can say to your children.

In reading this book to your child, I want you to see yourself as holding the space for your child's greatness. I believe a parent's job is to do this every day. Holding the space simply means intending the very best for your child, taking a deep breath, looking your child in the eyes and being very present with them (no distractions).

What is your goal for your child during this time? What do you want for them long-term? What do you want for your relationship with your children long-term? Please take a few minutes now and write these things down, prior to reading this story to your child.

Remember this does NOT have to be perfect. The most important thing is that your child knows you love them and will help them through this time. This will mean the world to your child.

What you may want to say or add to certain pages:

Page 7: You can add *we were so happy when you were born*.

Page 9: You can add anything about your child and what happened when they were small or anything about them *you were happy, cute and so fun*.

Page 15: You can add *some days Little Bear will live with OR visit Mama Bear and some days Little Bear will live with OR visit Daddy Bear*. Please revise this as it relates to your family. You can point to the two different caves and the path, as you say this.

Page 21: Pause here and listen. Be ready to say, *that is a good question*. This may open up a discussion. You may also not know the answer to their question, so you can say *let us get back to you about that*. You can also say after their first question, *what else might he/she have a question about*?

Page 23: If they can't read, read through the words for them. If they answer "scared", you can say *why might Little Bear feel scared?* You can do this with any question. You can tell your child *it is totally OK to feel sad. Sometimes, mommy/daddy feels sad, happy, frustrated (etc.) too*. You can say whatever feelings your child says here. You could also ask them here using any other emotion (i.e. scared, worried, upset) *what could he do to feel better, if he feels that way?*

Page 24: You can give your child ideas here: *Could Little Bear hug his stuffy or his mom or dad? Maybe he could tell his parents or his teacher, or he could go outside and play. It is totally fine to feel sad. Even mommy/daddy feels sad sometimes.*

Page 25: You can give your child ideas here: *Maybe he could take deep breaths, jump up and down or put his anger in a box.*

Page 29: Whisper these things in your child's ear. They love this but don't say it is a secret. It is not good for children to think they should keep things a secret.

You can ask them after the second bullet (if this is not the first time you have spoken to your child about divorce): *Have you ever felt like the divorce was your fault?* If they say yes, you ask *what would make you feel that way?* You could then say, *nope, divorce is never, ever a kid's fault. Divorce is always an adult choice that has nothing to do with the children.* You can also add anything here that you believe is important for your children to know. If this is the first time you have spoken to your child about divorce, wait and ask this question about them feeling that divorce is their fault at some point in the future.

Page 33: Make sure that you are at eye level with your child and listen. Once your child tells you what they think Mama Bear and Daddy Bear can do, say to them, *those are great ideas, thank you.* I know it can feel challenging to see this positive picture but it truly is what you want to intend for the future. You want to intend a healthy relationship with your co-parent.

Page 34: Last Comments to Your Child:

You can decide what you want to say here. You can choose to say any of the following to your child. Be sure to be on their level and look them in the eyes.

- *Please always tell me if I can do anything to help you or make you feel better.*
- *Do you need anything from me right now?*
- *I want you to know that I am so glad you love your mom/dad (your co-parent, your child's other parent).*
- *I am so grateful for your mommy/daddy because _____ insert positive characteristic about your co-parent (i.e., has a good job and works hard, is fun, is a good cook, loves you so much, is so patient with you, is so great at helping you with school, teaches you to_____).*
- *Give them a HUGE hug and tell them how much you love them and will love them forever.*

Future Conversations with Your Child: When your child brings you something (even if it is a frustration with your co-parent) simply say to them: **How are you doing?** and then say, **How can I support you?** These two questions are very helpful for children to hear from their parents. They can be used in almost any challenging situation you encounter with your child.

You will do great. Please reach out if I can help your family in any way. I also offer parent/older children's sessions via Zoom or phone www.healthychildrenofdivorce.com.

If *Little Bear and the Two Caves* helped your family, could you take a quick minute to help other kids and leave a review on Amazon? If you have improvement suggestions, please email us directly at healthychildrenofdivorce@gmail.com.

Scan the code or click the link below:

Thank you!
Shannon Rios Paulsen MS LMFT PCC
www.healthychildrenofdivorce.com

Little Bear and The Two Caves

by Shannon R Rios Paulsen
MS LMFT PCC

A Children's Book About Divorce with a Parent's Guide to Help Children Understand and Talk About Divorce

Illustration by Ayan Saha

Mama Bear and Daddy Bear lived in a cave.

One day, they were given the best gift in the world: a Baby Bear. That's YOU! They were so happy when Baby Bear was born.

When Baby Bear arrived in the cave they were so happy! They danced, sang and loved Baby Bear to the moon.

They went on walks, found honey and went fishing. Baby Bear grew up to be a Little Bear!

One day, Mama Bear and Daddy Bear realized they had different needs and decided to live in separate caves.

When Mama Bear lives in her own cave and Daddy Bear lives in his own cave, it is called divorce.

Little Bear will now live in two caves. Little Bear will go back and forth between Mama Bear's cave and Daddy Bear's cave.

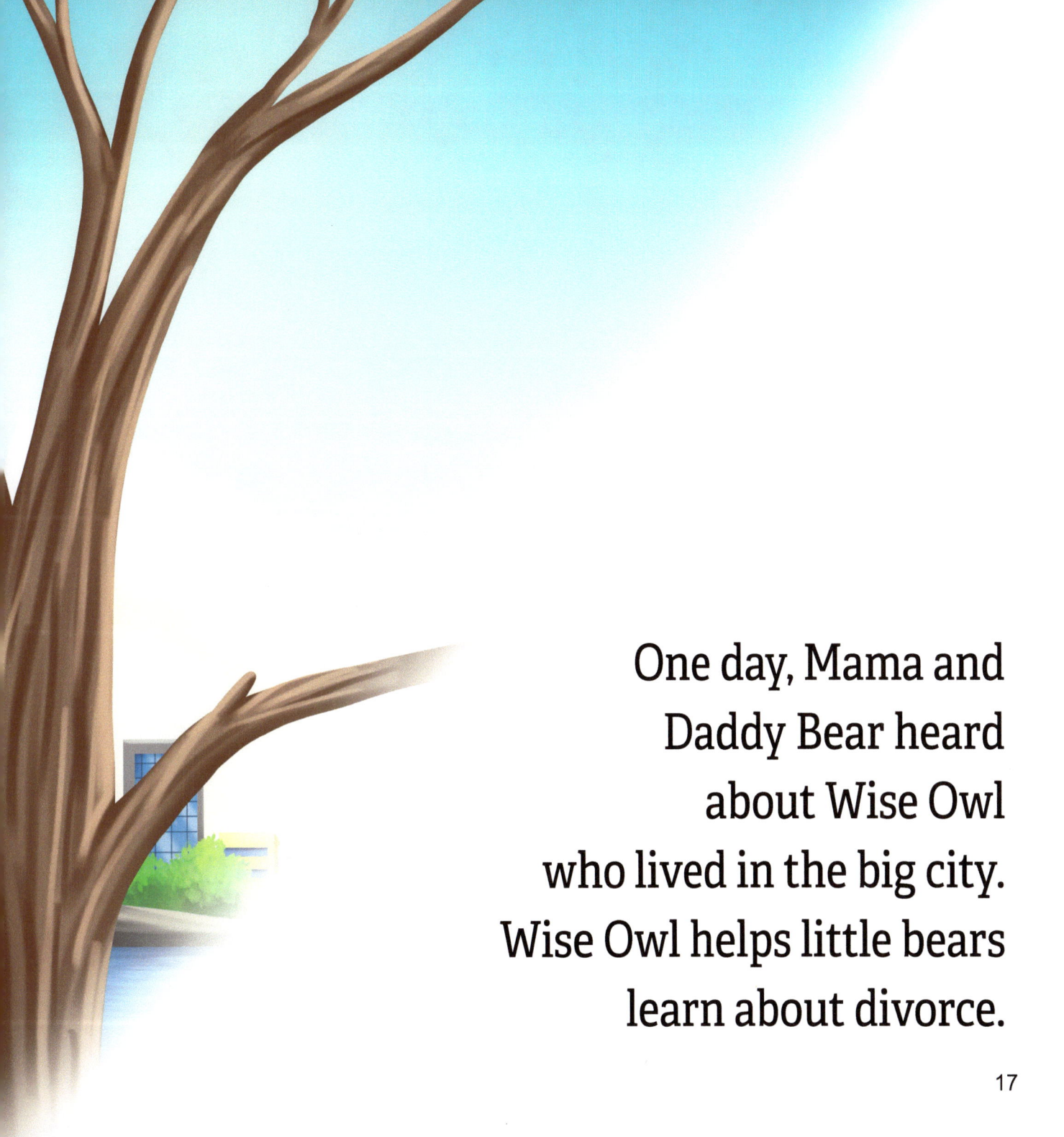

One day, Mama and Daddy Bear heard about Wise Owl who lived in the big city. Wise Owl helps little bears learn about divorce.

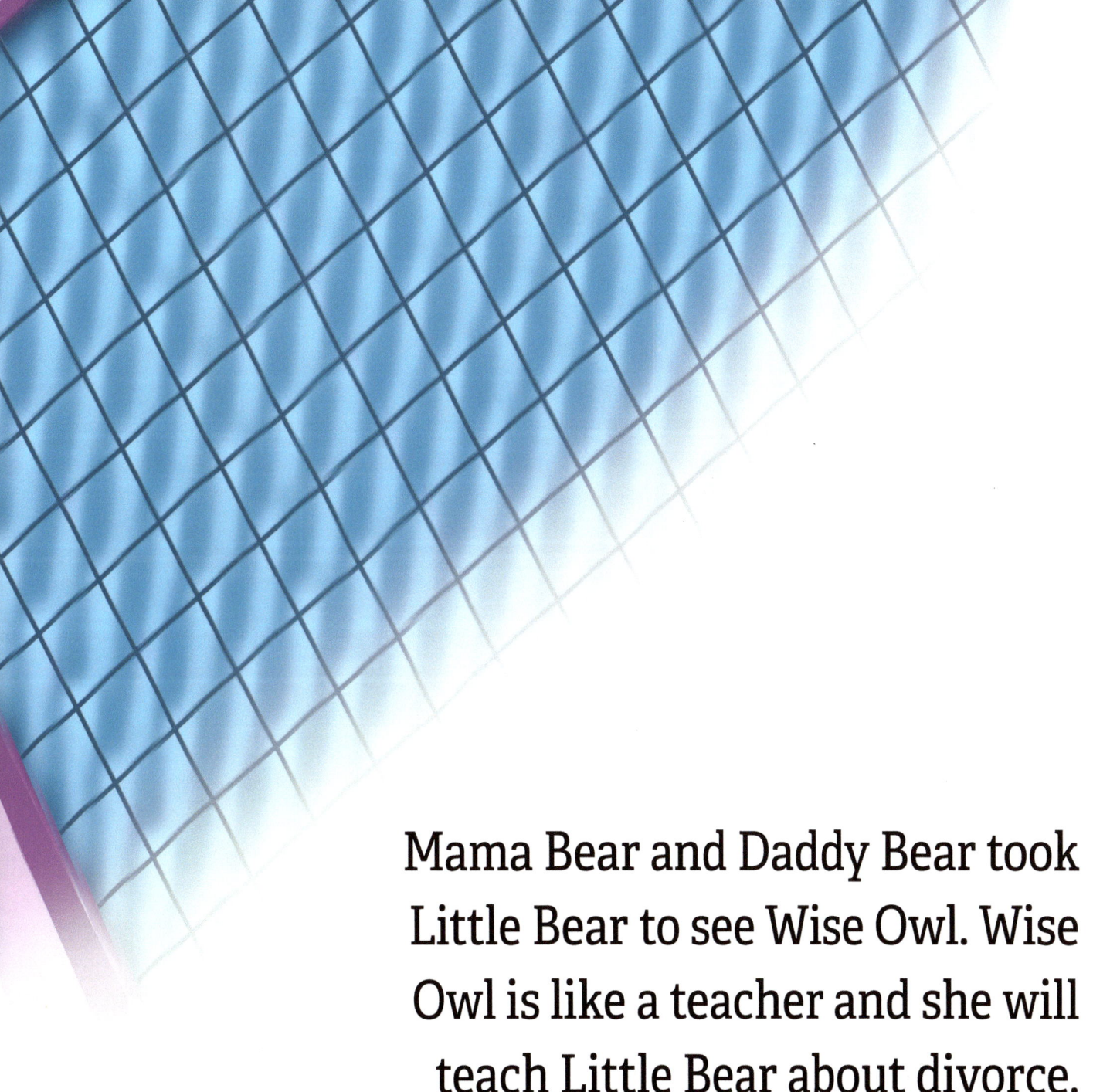

Mama Bear and Daddy Bear took Little Bear to see Wise Owl. Wise Owl is like a teacher and she will teach Little Bear about divorce.

What questions do you think Little Bear might have about divorce? What worries might Little Bear have?

How do you think Little Bear might feel about the divorce?

Worried	Happy	Scared

OK	Sad	Excited

Angry	Good	Upset

If Little Bear feels sad, what could Little Bear do to feel better?
Is it OK to feel sad sometimes?

If Little Bear feels angry, what could Little Bear do to feel better? Do you think Little Bear could tell his/her Mom or Dad?

Little Bear had so much fun with Wise Owl. They played games and talked about how very strong Little Bear is.

Then Wise Owl whispered in Little Bear's ear some very important things about divorce. Do you want to hear them, too?

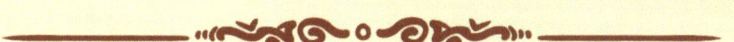

- Your parents will always love you, forever and ever. Mama Bear and Daddy Bear will always love you.

- You are an awesome Little Bear.
  You did not do anything wrong.
  Divorce is NEVER EVER a Little Bear's fault.

- You can always ask your parents any questions you have about divorce.

- You will always be with your parents (especially in their hearts), even if you're in different caves.

Little Bear was so happy he got to meet Wise Owl. She was smart and fun! He was happy he learned so much about divorce and he skipped all the way home.

What do you think
Little Bear's parents
could do to help
Little Bear feel safe and
happy during this time?
What could Mama Bear do?
What could Daddy Bear do?

Little Bear is feeling happy now because:

- Little Bear gets to see both of his/her parents.

- Little Bear brings his/her favorite toys and games back and forth to both caves.

- Little Bear's parents seem happier now.

- Little Bear knows the divorce was not her/his fault.

- Little Bear knows Mama Bear and Daddy Bear love him/her. They just had to live in separate caves.

- Little Bear's parents will love him/her forever.

Dear Reader,

My hope is that Little Bear and the Two Caves helped your family in a meaningful way. You can reach me directly at healthychildrenofdivorce@gmail.com with any improvement suggestions.

I would be so grateful if you could take a moment to leave a review on Amazon. Your feedback will help other families find this book and provide children with the support they need during this time.

Scan the code or click the link below to leave your review (if you purchased the book you can go to your Amazon page directly):

Thank you for helping me reach more families and make a difference, one child at a time!

With Love and Appreciation from my heart to yours,
Shannon Rios Paulsen MS LMFT PCC
Author of *Little Bear and the Two Caves*
www.healthychildrenofdivorce.com

Draw a Picture About Divorce.

Draw Your Feelings Here About Divorce.

Draw What You Can Do to Feel Happy.

www.ingramcontent.com/pod-product-compliance
Lightning Source LLC
Chambersburg PA
CBHW060821090426
42738CB00002B/69